Word Bird's™

Watch Out,
Word Bird!

Published in the United States of America by The Child's World®, Inc.
PO Box 326
Chanhassen, MN 55317-0326
800-599-READ
www.childsworld.com

Project Manager Mary Berendes
Editor Katherine Stevenson, Ph.D.
Designer Ian Butterworth

Library of Congress Cataloging-in-Publication Data
Moncure, Jane Belk.
Watch out, Word Bird! / by Jane Belk Moncure.
p. cm.
Summary: Word Bird learns a lesson in safety
when he disobeys his mother.
ISBN 1-56766-992-1 (lib. : alk. paper)
[1. Birds—Fiction.]   I. Title.
PZ7.M739 Wat 2002
[E]—dc21
2001006057

Word Bird's

Watch Out, Word Bird!

by Jane Belk Moncure

illustrated by Chris McEwan

One Day, Mama Bird said,
"Stay and play in the yard."

But Word Bird did not
stay in the yard.

Word Bird hopped down
the street…

to the park.

"I can swing,"
Word Bird said.

But Word Bird did
not see Cat.

Cat pushed Word Bird
up, up, up.

"Stop, Cat. I do not like
that," Word Bird said.

Word Bird climbed
up the slide.

Cat pushed Word Bird down,

down, down.

"Stop, Cat. I do not like that."

Word Bird sat on the seesaw.

Cat sat on the other end.

They went

up

and

down.

Then Cat bumped.

Bump,

bump.

"Stop, Cat. I do not like that."

Word Bird jumped
into the sandbox.

Cat threw sand
on Word Bird.

"Stop, Cat. I do not like that."

Cat grinned…

and came closer.

Word Bird saw Cat's teeth.

"Stop, Cat!" Word Bird said.

Cat came close,

so close...

Word Bird could feel Cat's whiskers!

Just then, Dog came by.

"Hi, Cat," Dog said.

"Bye-bye!" said Cat.

Word Bird hopped home
very, very fast.

Did Word Bird stay and
play in the yard? Yes!

Can you read these words with Word Bird?

yard

street

park

swing

up

cat

slide

seesaw

down

sandbox

teeth

whiskers

dog

Bye-bye!

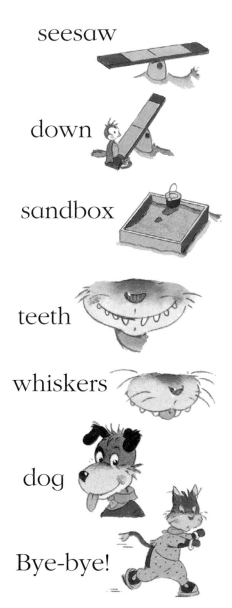